A Used Friend For Sale

My Poetry…

My Thoughts…

My Photography…

A Used Friend For Sale

COPYRIGHT 2007 By Devalle. All rights reserved

ISBN 978-0-6151-7807-3

Although this is poetry from my life experiences, the names, characters, places and incidents either are the product of the author's imagination.

All photos are copyright by Devalle, except theOld Golden Trumpet, Matthias Ebert, copyright 2007, and Alaknanda (Star in the window), Harneet Bhatia, copyright 2007.

To the one who's brought me closer to God...

If I have to, I can do anything...

I am strong...

I am invincible…

I am devalle

Metaphorically, in some fashion we are all articles in a yard sale. We are those articles at some point in our lives when we are unappreciated, lost or simply forgotten.

We are more than the baby doll that some little girl out grew. We are more than the baseball lost in an over-grown grassy field. It is our hope that on one sunny day, someone will pay the price to see us for who we really are.

So the question becomes, how do we become brand new again? My father once told me, one man's trash is another man's treasure. Perhaps this is how we are to feel brand new.

In my mind we are all used, and the love of others helps us to feel brand new again. It's when you meet someone for the first time and they know nothing of your pain, your past or your shortcomings. The only thing they see is a beautiful smile, an amazing personality, and a joyful soul.

Better yet, it's when a child says to his father, "you're my hero, even if you can't read me my favorite book". It is the lost souls who submerge themselves under water to cleanse or renew their faith in the presence of witnesses.

So here we are sitting in a yard sale. We are the painted picture whose colors are faded because the owner chose to leave us out in the sun for too long. We are the television that was traded in for the new thinner model, whose colors are no better than ours.

For now we are to enjoy the beautiful green lawns that we have the privilege to lie on. Enjoy the people as they rummage through the boxes as they decide if there's a place for us in their life. Enjoy the sun or the rain because we know, sooner rather than later, the right person will come and give us shelter or place us upon a mantle. Most importantly, enjoy the fact that we know being used is nothing more than an advantage over those things that are not.

So what is a used friend for sale?

Experience…Valuable…Classic…simply put, we are beautiful.

God has to be all things to all people

Anything less from you would be less than perfect

What we believe isn't as important as believing with faith

But you can't wait too long

Because you just might find yourself believing in nothing

And nothing is something the Lord would never want you to believe in

You all laugh at me because I am different, I laugh at you because you are all the same.

I stand as the background,

Black, in the middle of the planets

that revolves to my intellective

because I'm universal.

I don't wish upon stars, trinkets or wells

but all that I am...the Sun,

placed in the middle, my intellection

is what they circle.

To asks my color insults the

equilibrium that balances my creed,

by which makes me whole.

If you're going to ask my color,

make sure you judge my intelligence.

Black is the color of the Cosmo.

So doesn't that make me universal?

the life I live is no Shakespeare...

I Am No Loner

I am no loner due to loneliness being a good friend
I don't walk down roads already walked due to my knowing where they will
end
I don't show my feelings due to my feelings being my enemy
And I'll never buy her shoes because she could one day walk out on me

What I am is a realist because the life I live is no Shakespeare
What enters my thoughts controls my mind, so I make sure to keep them
clear
I find being proud is no longer a good thing but I take pride in all that I do
And learning to draw is using all colors, and no longer relying on blue

Who am I? I'm a man that many think they are
Where do I want to go? Anywhere because nowhere is not too far
My life is not wishing upon the stars but the sun that gives life to the day
That larger is not always best but for me it's the only way

So I am no loner due to the fact that loneliness is a good friend
I don't intend to ever write a book if I don't already know how it will end
For my future knows in the present that all my answers lie in the past
And the choices I make are the ones that will forever last

Is It A Sunday?

Down from your hometown I wait
impatiently for your call
I find myself in this position more now
Just a fool in composition…that's all

Back in Houston, down the street on Richmond
my best friend waits for me
Living a double Lfe far from what I ever wanted;
I'm living a life of jeopardy

A quarter pass four in the morning
I can't find comfort from sleep
My dreams war with my reality
of everything I ever wanted
And my skeleton's crumble from my closet
since there's no room to hang,
telling myself it's a Sunday
But I know much better than this,
as I grip my anger with my fist
because I should have known it was a Monday

Ersatz Tears

Who are we to place judgment?

Who am I to try and purify?

Ersatz Tears, no pearls fall from my eyes

I am who I am, surrounded by lies

But is it silly to think that a man's truly happy when he dies?

Who are we to convict?

Who am I to rectify?

We are who we are, full of our own demises

Yes, but I don't know why

Why it is that we don't know how to fly

What I would do is what you should do

if your eyes mimic mine than there is time

If we all just learn to try

Bucket Of Rain

"Helpless living with concrete windows
Careless innuendoes without the severity"

Is the world against me? It feels like I'm falling
There are many heavens but I can't seem to find the one for me…
my seven now appears to be eleven
I circle the stars to find the distance Mars,
Sun of tranquility is close but yet it's still too far

I don't know much but I do know what I'm going through
A lesson learned? If not me then who?
I don't know much but I know my own pains
Life for what it's worth is a bucket of rain

To say, "just live you life" would be a contradictory
because with my dreams I can't conquer the world with simple miracles
It's just another deception that's far from reality
of all the things I've ever wanted to be
But the key to our laughter is nothing more than a circus of our failures
disguised as clowns to celebrate who we really are
I don't know much but I do know my own pain
Life for what it's worth is a bucket of rain

My Brother

Does anyone know who's my brother
in this land that labels by color?
I was told that it's hard to get passed my hue
and it was God's way of saying, "I hate you"

Can you please tell me if you're my brother?
My mother was told by television shepherds you were
and that's what I learned from her
I guess with all the confusion, no one bothers
to be my brother

Does it matter that my brother is not my color?
Some say he's a traitor for being brothers with a nigger
So is that the problem with this land that labels by color?
Is that why my brother doesn't bother?

Please Don't Throw Away The Bottle

I find it hard to make it home

crossing the street has become more of a chore

Whereas my wife only cares to be alone

and the sound it God awful from the hedges

when I walk through the door

So please don't throw away the bottle

I need it to enjoy the rain

And I may no seem like much in the eyes of others

but at least they know my name

When I drive I can't see the lines

not sure if I'm intoxicated or just under the influence

But all is well and all is mine

and the sound is God awful from my inebriated conscience

So please don't throw away the bottle

I think I'm going to need it now

I may not seem like much in the eyes of others

but I know in time I'll find my joyful sound

My watch no longer works

The only time I know remains at a quarter pass three

So I drift with the wind because that's all I'm worth

and sound that is God awful is the Lord calling for me

So please don't throw away the bottle

I need it to help me with the pain

And I'm not much in the eyes of others

but at least they know my name

The Man From Providence

Trying to pray upon the stars
searching for who we are
like a fool who no longer wants to be a clown
Looking between the silver moon and the distance Mars
deep down you always knew it's harder to go up than to come down

Sometimes we cry with the rain,
falling all the same are the tears…I wonder
The man up the street sleeps on the concrete
they say he's a mishap of his own beliefs…I wonder

The old man he's from Providence
where he lived with no residence,
says he wants to live a better life
He walks the street in dirty clothes
but at least he knows the difference between wrong and right
He holds his hand in front of me;
I have what he needs but he makes me nervous
As I walk by I don't know why
but he smiles and thanks Jesus

On the main street we just pass him by
without a care in the world
and I don't know why
Why it is we can't understand the difference
between hello and goodbye

The old man walks to his favorite spot,

as the people laugh in his face

and take cheap shots;

he only forgives them for their ignorance

He tries to find his favorite star

and for some reason he's all nervous

He smiles between the silver moon and the distance Mars

And says, "My time is close to seeing Jesus"

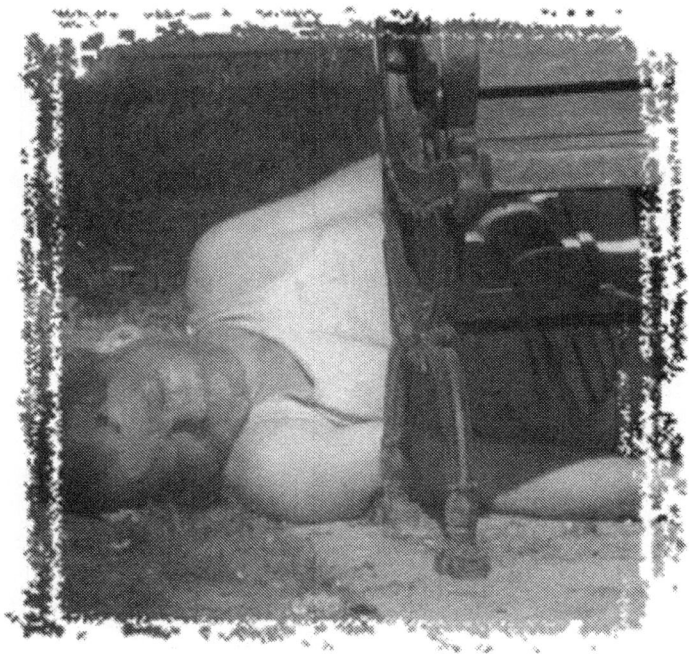

Thoughts Of A Sometimes Lonely Derelict

Goodbye, goodbye
I slip onto the streets of Houston
walking pass people sleeping on dirty sideways
wondering their Lfe before and where it went wrong

What's five dollars to me?
Or better yet, does it make me a better human being?
I see the rain falling faster and faster
asking myself, what does it all mean?

I journey through back alleys, cardboard boxes and no hope
Where then do they turn after being labeled a derelict?
"May god bless you" is all that I hear
and it's so, so

Goodbye, goodbye is their diction
because they know a face is nothing more than a billboard
that reads, "it's you own fault for you're dereliction"

Last November

If you knew there would be no more summers
How would you feel? What would you have done?
Would you tell your mother you loved her?
Would you take time to watch the swans serenade the Crystal Pond?

If you knew this would be your last September
What would you do different?
Would you keep your promise, if only you remembered?
Would you sit down with your father hoping to make a difference?

If you knew this would be your last December snow
What would you do?
Could you learn a silent prayer for all to know?
Or would you rather ask forgiveness for all the years you chose not too?

If this was the last rain in April's spring
How would you change your day?
Would help those in need learn to sing?
Better yet, share your ice cream on a Strawberry Sunday

We are nothing more than who we've framed ourselves
Choosing gold over silver not knowing there's no difference
What we are isn't as important as being someone of reverence
Finding salvation in the last hours is now a competition

If this is my last November
What would I do?
I'd stand next to the one who's falling
Never wondering if it could one day be you

Please Don't Betray Me

Two young at heart, learning with the soul, as the blustery weather
directed us in a position unfamiliar
I stood alone for so long, I believe only in myself that
constancy was the look when I laid my eyes on her
Now we all have our reveries of make believes that we
truly have to believe with some kind of loyalty
As we embraced, I believed in only us,
imploring that you 'please don't betray me'

Now I believe you love not with the heart but with your soul
because the soul is the salvation that makes us whole
Never put your faith in change because your heart will eventually change,
as she left I felt the alleviation of now loving with the soul
Standing in the wintry weather not knowing that it's Fall
I saw the signs but was too afraid of being alone…
I hoped for some sort of loyalty
Not knowing if we will make love, as I laid in a dense haze
praying the recognizable truth…she'd just betrayed me

All I ask is that you stand with serenity and loyalty
And in time, my heart you will cultivate thee
But I implore 'please just don't betray me'

A Sailor At Sea

Under a sea of unforgiving blue,

tell me where might I find you?

As beautiful as the day, I see only shades of gray

that's innuendo blue

Everyday is the same day,

where every Sunday is a Monday

The smell of cold steel,

waiting I guess for the signs of a beautiful Wednesday

As we all look the same,

looking around a few have the same last name

But why do we do this?

Salt water, smelly fish; why in heaven do we do this?

I

t's sometimes lonely with a poet's mind

to make acceptance with peace

God calls and the other's run

but I'm already there to be release

Time flies when you're sleep

embracing every dream knowing it'll end

And I see and hear things that wonder

if anyone here knows about sin

Yeah, it's funny how time flies

even when it's time to take a warm shower

What does another country has that my living room doesn't?

A view of the Eiffel Tower?!

It's time for home.

It's time for the warmth my bed and the laughter of my child

It's time for real food and a cold Rolling Rock...

It's time simply to smile

No more hard steel and demeaning gestures by idiots

telling me to be here or there

Just my old lady and I,

lying close, as I run my fingers through her hair

Yeah, this is what life is,

the details,

not sweating the small...ssh...

And as I look at the unforgiving sea of blue,

I'm wondering why in heaven do we do this?

My Rainy Day With Miles Davis

Do you hear the music? Or can you hear the pain?

It's often in the reflection of falling tears.

It's well noted…its rain.

Can you taste the sincerity of every drop

that indents the earth with someone's dream?

Rain; it's famous that with every falling pearl there's

another that follows,

just not quite the same.

Rain falls in all motions

but only comes from one direction

taking shape in little unimportant oceans.

Rain, it comes and goes.

Where? I'm not sure if anyone knows

but we've all fallen in its puddles.

Do you hear the music? Or do you hear the rain?

Regardless of what you hear

someone feels pain in the midst of all this rain.

Musical it is

but it seems like a Melancholy Shade of Blue.

Good or Bad? Possibly even tad?

It's all astounded with the supremacy

of Miles Davis's Bitches Brew.

So is it rain or just another rainy day?

And if you hear music

I hope you hear Miles making love to his

trumpet in a Silent Way.

You'll need more than the sun if you want to me come judgment day...

Trust Yourself With Loving Me Baby

I'm not the little lady you met a few years back
You met me when you were on bending knees
Now I'm the time that occupies your mind
and as long as I'm inside you're never in need

So you can trust yourself with loving me baby

Trust the rain that I'm sending your way

Trust yourself with loving me baby

Because you'll need more than the sun

if you want to meet me come judgment day

I'll never change your mind baby

with your mind it would be easy

So I'll offer you my hand;

All you have to do is call for me

and know that I'll never change your mind baby

because changing your mind would be too easy

So trust yourself with loving me baby

Trust the rain I'll send for your garden

Trust yourself with loving me baby

Because you'll need more than the sun

If you want to meet me at the place where it all started

You're not the man you were a few years back

It would be impossible; my word is too strong

I'm the grapes of your vine baby

As long as I'm inside,

No one will do you harm

So trust yourself with loving me baby

Trust the rain that I'm sending your way

Trust yourself with loving me baby

Because you'll need more than the sun

If you want to me come judgment day

Michael's War

Believing in me is your protective armor
for the war-cry of Michael's armies
Your faith is your heavenly sword
for those spirits that won't go easy
Don't worry about piercing armor
salvation won't allow what they are striking for
Some may come in single file lines
Some will fall to my mighty hand
Some will come to recognize a beautiful mind
Some the execution of felling to understand
You can't go on having faith in the world
But have faith you can fight in Michael's war
And you can't go on believing
something other than me is what you're fighting for

So make sure to believe in your protective armor
I need you in Michael's army
Your faith is your heavenly sword
For those spirits that won't fall easy
And don't worry about piercing armor
I won't allow them to strike what they're aiming for
Some will come to believe
Some will make a place for me at the table
Some will have no choice but to leave
Some will be willing but forgiven because they're not able
So don't put your faith in others
But believe you're a part of Michael's war
And you can't succeed if you're believing
Something other than me is what you're fighting for

My Coat-Hangar Halo

Try to understand me
and don't amend what I'm saying
Where I'm from and who I am
you wouldn't understand
So just see me…
just see me from where I stand
Just see me…
just see me for who I am
Contentment came from the days when you were young
even if you didn't understand
The sun shines because it's time
and it doesn't really give a damn
So I wonder…
I wonder if heaven has any place to be
Because I've notice…
I've notice this world has no place for me

Don't worry because there's no need too
just take the time to get to know me
Because who I am and where I'm from
you just might disagree
So just see me…
just see me as someone you'd like to know
Can you see it?
Can you see my coat-hangar halo?
And I wonder…
I wonder if heaven's in a rush to see me
Because I've notice…
I've notice this world is too much of a mystery

...for I'm a mold from your clay

Ode to Henry and Hazel

Henry will you remember that I was your grandson
even if I no longer resemble my father?
And would you believe that I'm the man of a little one
even though she looks more like her mother?

And if you could believe her eyes are full of Hazel
but I consider them to be brown and pretty plain
And she's not like you, more on the move like Hazel
But her smile is far from ordinary, a lot like Betty Jane

Everyday is the same old Monday,
Hazel shouting at Henry from the porch
But he can't hear she's only asking about his day
and a little about Judge Wagner's verdict on the People's Court

Sitting on Red Oak you can smell the smoke from his lungs
and hear Hazel's same ole song about those damn cigarettes
Walking to his Lincoln he's teased by the calm breeze of falling leaves
saying, "How about is shade tree instead of Jeanerette"

And if you could believe her eyes are full of Hazel
but I consider them to be brown and pretty plain
And she's nothing like you; on the move like Hazel
but her smile is far from ordinary, a lot like Betty Jane

You Are My Father

I wonder where you are going

with once was a handsome face now pulling down

You fade away to things you can't remember

but can smell and sound

I am your Gardener

I am a Shepherd for the one who has all the answers for you

You are my father that's for sure

And I do know where you are going is where I someday hope to be

I wonder where you are going

You ask me for answers

to questions of where you are, how long and how far

And along the way

you grew weaker but you can rest on me

for I'm a mold from your clay

I am your brightest color

I am a Shepherd to the one who commands me to stand with you

You are my father for all to see

And I do know where you are going is where I fight to be

I wonder where you are going

With an unfamiliar face with tears where your smile is lost

But you are my father forever and knowing

that I am a Shepherd to the one who commands me to carry you to the cross

I'm your Greeter

and a Shepherd to many

But you are my father that's for sure

And I do know where you're going is where I hope to be

Dead Tree In Cedar Bayou

I watch life from a window I can't see
Hasty, yet lengthy, my face is no longer my identity
The night's shadows and voices are playing tricks on me
I guess this damn cancer won't let me be
Medication mutilating my genes, yet it can't mass the pain
Laying on either side the pain's still the same

Here now I lay wondering if this is a test of my faith
Are the angels white? And will he even let me through the gate?
The night's shadows and voices are playing tricks on me
And this damn cancer…it won't let me be
And I can't make out who's calling my name
Could it be my brother?…Hazel…Henry…or Betty Jane?

They ask me how does it feel?
How does the medication make your feel?
Please don't ask me how I feel…
I feel alone and my mind won't tell me what's real
So please asks me how do you do?
And I'll smile and tell you,
I feel like a dead tree I use to stare at
down in Cedar Bayou

Old Sky Blue Chevy

I can't see the colors of my rainbow
But I know I saw them not long ago
I may not know how wide the size or the trim
But I know the sky blue of your old Chevy was one of them

Stop for me if you're going home
I want to ride on the passenger side
Windows rolled down and the wind against me
I miss riding in your old sky blue Chevy

All I care to know is my father's favorite fishing hole
And the Big Red putting up a fight on his old fishing pole
Memories of his smile are framed and kept in my home
Leaving me a little afraid to delete his number from my cell phone

So stop for me if you're going home
I want to ride on the passenger side
Windows down with the wind against me
I miss the smell of your old sky blue Chevy

I can't see the colors of my rainbow
No more Cracker Jacks and Astros
Just the reflection of what he was upon my face
No more weekends at his place

So stop for me if you're going home
I want to ride on the passenger side
The wind, my old man and me
Turning the curve on Magnolia in his old sky blue Chevy

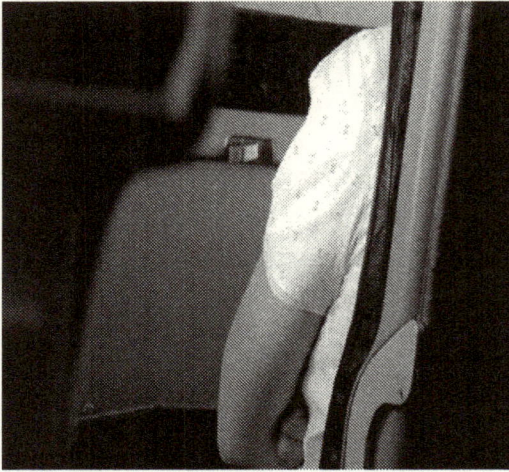

Matilda's Baby

She takes a look out the back window like a child into a world

that doesn't know if she's black or pale

Between the hues of a better view, she reads the want ads

for a used friends for sale

As I take in the breeze between Fall and Spring

Where it comes from I'm not sure...

She says she's sorry, as her tears scream to the floor

Why she apologizes, I'm not sure...

Matilda's long from Lafayette,

barely speaking any English

but in love with a thin man name Willie

When she talks it's pretty edgy

with flowing white hair,

like the clouds when it touches the city

Willie opens the door

takes off his clothes

Could it be his way of getting close

with Jesus?
Matilda cry's and recognizes
his time has come,
as she brings him in and thanks him for his serve

(Matilda says to her babies)
"Come on home baby,
don't sleep like the weary children
who flow with the outward wind"
Matilda tells her baby to
get it together and know
Willie didn't die for nothing

Shh, she tells her baby
"don't let him toy with your mind"
She says, "Mom, I know. This time
he understands"
But he waits in his car
in the parking lot
"no more cheap shots…
it's got to stop!"
as she places her bags
in his gray sedan

As she looks out the window
She see his reflections of emptiness
because with him she can never tell
Reading the want ads she
wonders and wonders if she has
enough courage to purchase a
used friend for sale?

Nod Street

Trying to find the way that leads
to the empty lot on Nod Street
I take the Highlands and pass the cemetery
just before entering town
Driving pass the monsters, as they sleep
gently on the cold and bruised concrete
And my linage, which grows on a tree...
like apples falling to the ground

I turn the corner that leads back to
the fig tree at the end of Nod Street
All the memories of my childhood
I still breath in the air
As though I'd never
stopped living there
Even now I take pride where the
roots and the ground meet
and when my head is above the clouds
I'm reminded of life on Nod Street

Can someone tell me if the lot is still
empty on Nod Street?
Nothing more than memories of
a boy just being a boy
And friends that are now lost
to the outward current of the sea
While the empty lot of my former
still lives where the ground and roots
brings life to the fig tree

Lily's A Little Jealous

Maddie's new doll she named Charlotte
Her old doll Lily is now a little jealous
Tea parties, sleepovers, playtime and joyrides
Ms. Lily is no longer allow to play outside
She tucks Charlotte under the covers with a nighttime kiss
While Lily's tucked away in the toy box; she didn't make the list

Now Maddie like's to play with her new ones
The old ones she tends to keep on the shelf
Maddie's so young; she believes their all having fun
Does she really believe they are all in touch?

You would never believe that Ms. Lily was once Charlotte
Never would you believe she was once just as cool
And you'll start to believe that Lily is a little jealous
of Charlotte's lipstick and rouge

Maddie wants to bring Charlotte to Sabbath's show and tell
Because Lily already knows the story of Jonah in the belly of the whale
The tears in her eyes as she leaves her new friend behind
Ms. Lily has a smirk. She knows it's only a matter of time

Now Maddie loves to play with her new ones
The old ones she leaves all alone on the shelf
So young and naïve, she believes they're having fun
Does she really think Charlotte feels her touch?

My father once told me,

"that friends will come and go.

The ones you think are you friends

tell you they'll be there but never show.

Your friends you see...

(holding up two fingers)

you can count with a peace sign

one...two...

You're always your first friend,

along with that Hispanic boy too."

My Peace Sign

There was a lot to do in the middle of the week
Broke down, steam forming clouds in the middle of the street
Never a bored moment with my peace sign
City Streets, Magic Bus and a long line at Strict Nine

I can always rely on my peace sign but he's never on time
Drinking E&J from a faded cup with a splash of lime
Watching Friday all night on a Saturday just-a-clowin'
Heading to the club in the middle of storm…car nearly drowin'

Yeah me and my peace sign was never far from the scene
Hiding the fact we didn't have any money by dressing so clean
Bobbing our heads to Tupac and Biggie giving props from way back
And sing out loud, "I got 5 on it, podna…let's go half on a sack"

Uh-huh, my peace sign was bright and always flashing in neon
Creeping real slow, choking down the bitter taste of the Red Elephant
Being the first in the club and yet we still made a scene
Fore-day in the morning, passing Budweiser smelling green beans

Yes sir, my peace sign was from the old and never from the new
Walking out the club yelling, "who got 7-2?"
In the reflection from the skylines was a high-speed of red
Looking over at my peace sign, "What'd up Craig?"

My imagination of you....

Down on Luck Again

Tell me how to understand
How never to lose what I've found
How to walk as an Honest Man
And how never to forget my Joyful Sound

Never want to go back to when love was wrong
How never to live short when the days are long
Can you teach me how to be what you are in my eyes?
Show me the right way, the only way to be at your side
Tell me a fairytale. Tell me how it should end
Can we go to the movies and cry together
Because I'm down on luck again

I have more lonely nights then peaceful ones
There are times when I hear you laughing,
other times I hear nothing
And more often I'm a hero who's song goes unsung
But as long as you're near
in this world I am someone

Never want to look back to when love was wrong
I don't mind if my song goes unsung
Can you teach me how to be what you are in my eyes?
I don't mind if I never fly away in that special sky
Tell me a fairytale. Tell me how it should end
I need a little inspiration because
I'm down on luck again

The Elephant Cry's & The Eagle Screams

You saw every imperfection in me

but yet you never once took me from any of your dreams

Elephant cry's and the eagle screams

whenever you're not around it seems

Going nowhere fast and going very slow,

your never-ending belief in me continued to parade

While on my last stand in life you turned and gave me yours

not wanting to see me fade

To you I owe you my life;

every degree of my courage is devoted to you

and all that you stand for

You're the reason I exist

and the motivation to open and close any door

Deep between the valleys, rivers and streams

there I stood waiting for nothing;

I knew of nothing

Elephant continued to cry

and the screams were ever louder from the eagle it seems

Taking my hand into the gentleness of your palms

at that very moment I realized I was given anew

Not fearing which way to turn,

only turning to see you is the only turn

this lonely poet dares to do

To you I owe heaven; the only angel designed

to save me from this world of crazy fools

I now know the meaning of life,

only to have it recognized through the fantastic things you do

My Imagination Of You

Your composition is so very beautiful
that I want to feel myself lying next to you
The kindness of your kiss journeys beneath my skin
persuading my desires to experience the savor of your sweet nectar
that brings rapture to my tree of life
Heaven everlasting, the phone just wants to vice me more
that my imagination intensifies and my cup gushes full

Enduring I pause awaiting your summons
that I repeatedly illustrate conjuring up images of you
Where I'm in a war zone with my telephone
that I detect myself hurrying home
Your voice mesmerize my thoughts wanting me to do things
with you that I'm too introverted to say so you leave me to aspiration

I Am

In the view of your crystal waterfall…I hear sound

Under the flickering of your radiant Sun…I feel beautify

Entangled in the harmony of your gentle current…you I've found

Astonished by the sweetness of your breath…I am purified

The laughter of your smile…I am privileged

Gazing into your eyes…I am acclaimed

Simply knowing everything you do…I am up-lifted

You knowing of my imperfections and still be there…I feel no shame

Taking comfort in your shelter…I am anew

Placing me inside the middle of your love…I am at peace

Honor to stand at your shores grasping your waves…I am one with you

And the allure of your and I…I am released

7 Times By God's Wealth

This is my dedication to show you just how far you've brought me

You've shown me in your eyes everything I ever wanted to be

With every hour you've given me inspiration to move mountains with destiny

And if I was curse to be blind I'll never worry;

through your eyes I truly see

that

"You're the brightest color in my garden of flowers

You're the fines minute of my greatest hour

Into your eyes I could find

 a place, 7 times by God's wealth,

I could truly die."

I look to heaven knowing one day God would have me

But I realized without you I pray for an eternity

In darkness the light of your tranquility guides my eyes

and if I was curse to be blind I'll never worry;

through you I truly see

that

"You're the painted picture of how the world should be

You're the Northern Star of my university

You're the mighty Nile that run's along the Red Sea

And into your eyes I can truly find

a place, 7 times by God's wealth,

I could truly die."

The Small Of Her Back

He gently guides her through the crowd
with his hand on the small of her back.
With every look of her eyes he felt the first time
he'd place a sweet kiss on the collar of her neck.

As all the heads turn to witness this marvelous creature
with such refinement and charm
they wonder what was god thinking,
as he places his caressing hand on the smooth skin of her arm.
What splendor of nectar in this glorified woman's allure,
which would leave you speechless and out of breathe?
wondering if he could find love
as he placed another kiss on her shoulder
with his hand on the small of her back.

How do you praise a woman who's far beautiful

to even be allowed in heaven?

So independent it's simple sexy

when she turns and walks in.

He shows adoration to show dedication

that he guides her through the crowd

with his hand on the small of her back.

His every effort in life is to indulge in her,

as he continues his thoughts of the first kiss

on the collar of her neck.

This is the manner, by which he chose to exhibit

this gallery of compliments, to prove what she is in his eyes.

Love is no such a word to compare this feeling of

devotion that he must honor until the day,

which without her he must die.

With every pedal of his precious red rose

he bring forth his lips in his effort to capture the first kiss

he place upon the shoulders of her neck.

His head, like the flying flag of America,

feeling honor to walk side someone so breathtaking, as it is shown with his

hand at the small of her back.

These Questions

In the middle of spring I hear the birds whisper your name

With their wings expanding over a sea of unforgiving blue

Where are you from? And why are you not the same?

Where did you hide your halo? Is heaven as beautiful as you?

In my mind every picture of you is painted and framed

Where everything spoken are only 3 words, but I wonder if you will know?

Will you come if I call? If I told you would your remember my name?

Or care not to know? And will you accept my invitation to a silent show?

So at best I realize you're a flower in a garden that I want to glorify

Knowing this garden is nothing without the radiance of your sun rays

Tell me your best feature because I love them all? Tell me...tell me why?

Tell me which night...which night you love to wear your favorite negligee?

It's September now, and I only hear the leaves screaming your name

I'm the only one that can hear it, and it's so damn clear but I can't confide

Can you see you're the touch of a lifetime? Can you see you're not the same?

Can you see? Can you see I've always loved that halo you've tried to hide?

My Thoughts....

What is the future?

It's the very first step you take in predicting it!

Never try to explain yourself.
Because your true friends already know.
And your enemies…well…
they'll never believe it.

If you really think about it, why be like someone else? Try being yourself. Besides, everyone is already taken.

I will always own an umbrella. That way NO ONE can ever piss on my leg and tell me it's raining!

Don't be afraid of shadows. They're only there to let us know that light is

nearby.

Don't worry that children never listen to you.

Worry that they are always watching you.

Fear is the state of allowing your mind to fear darkness.

It's allowing your mind to picture a dark room

where negatives are developed…

If you want to fly like others,

try running off a cliff.

BUT if you want to soar above them,

try spreading your wings.

www.ingramcontent.com/pod-product-compliance
Lightning Source LLC
Chambersburg PA
CBHW021344090426
42742CB00008B/743